Tom Stephen & Virginia Starkey
Photos by Hank Foto

FEARLESS

Regal

From Gospel Light
Ventura, California, U.S.A.

Published by Regal Books
From Gospel Light
Ventura, California, U.S.A.

Regal Books is a ministry of Gospel Light, a Christian publisher dedicated to serving the local church. We believe God's vision for Gospel Light is to provide church leaders with biblical, user-friendly materials that will help them evangelize, disciple and minister to children, youth and families.

It is our prayer that this Regal book will help you discover biblical truth for your own life and help you meet the needs of others. May God richly bless you.

For a free catalog of resources from Regal Books/Gospel Light, please call your Christian supplier or contact us at 1-800-4-GOSPEL or www.regalbooks.com.

Cover and interior design by Josh Talbot Design (www. joshuatalbotdesign.com)

Library of Congress Cataloging-in-Publication Data
Stephen, Tom.
  Fearless / Tom Stephen and Virginia Starkey; photos by Hank Foto.
     p. cm.
  ISBN 0-8307-4295-6 (trade paper)
  1. Peace of mind—Religious aspects—Christianity—Meditations. 2. Fear—Religious aspects—Christianity—Meditations.
I. Starkey, Virginia. II. Title.
  BV4908.5.S75 2006
  242'.4—dc22
2006016524

Rights for publishing this book in other languages are contracted by Gospel Light Worldwide, the international nonprofit ministry of Gospel Light. Gospel Light Worldwide also provides publishing and technical assistance to international publishers dedicated to producing Sunday School and Vacation Bible School curricula and books in the languages of the world. For additional information, visit www.gospellightworldwide.org; write to Gospel Light Worldwide, P.O. Box 3875, Ventura, CA 93006; or send an e-mail to info@gospellightworldwide.org.

What do you fear? The dark? Terrorism? Loss of a job? Death?

Creation and God's Word tell us a simple truth:

No fear, God is near.

This book was written and photographed in memory of

Valentine James Stephen (1912-1992):

a man who faced life without fear and taught his children to do the same.

Introduction

The great Hawaiian ambassador and surfer Duke Kahanamoku taught a simple lesson about his relationship with the forces of nature: *Never turn your back on the ocean.* Contemplation of the waters of creation stimulates extreme emotion—a warm sunset over the island of Oahu inspires peace; a massive storm surge pounding the island's north shore demands fear and respect.

Jesus, the great ambassador of heaven, also taught a simple lesson: "Do not be afraid of those who kill the body and after that can do no more. Fear him who, after the killing of the body, has power to throw you into hell. . . . Are not five sparrows sold for two pennies? Yet not one of them is forgotten by God. Indeed, the very hairs of your head are all numbered. Don't be afraid; you are worth more than many sparrows" (Luke 12:4-7).

We are valuable to God, who has the power to give life or death to our souls. Although we know from God's Word how He cares for us, even so, we can imagine that Jesus might tell us, *Never turn your back on God.*

Do you want to live free from the anxiety that permeates most of society? Are you tired of being overly stressed about the circumstances in your life? This book invites you to turn toward God and find the freedom you seek.

For thousands of years, people have found freedom from fear as they have interacted with the ocean. As we reflect on the awe and fear that the ocean inspires, and if we slow down and listen with heart and soul, we can hear the voice of God.

However, God did not leave us to try to understand Him simply through His creation. He has also chosen to speak to us directly. The Scriptures of the Old and New Testament are the written accounts of God's interactions with people throughout history. For thousands of years, people like us have found freedom from fear as we sat quietly and listened to God's voice spoken through Scripture. The mysterious presence in creation becomes known through these ancient words.

Fearless: Reflecting on Life Without Fear was created to give you the opportunity to discover or deepen your relationship with God. Every day you will be given an image from the creative eye of an extreme water photographer as an aid to reflection and meditation. As you read, reflect and listen over the next 40 days, you will discern the voice of God through both word and image.

It is our hope that the use of both image and word will help you redirect your focus from the day-to-day grind and stress to the God who made you and loves you. As you reflect on these images and incorporate the words of God into your life, you will begin to experience moments of peace and learn to live life from a new perspective: *You have no need to fear; God is near.*

Discovering a life with God takes time and practice. That's why this book has been separated into 40 days. Noah spent 40 days being tossed around in the Flood until finally God brought peace to his family and the earth. Jesus spent 40 days in the desert preparing for His ministry. You, too, will have the chance to spend 40 days with God!

Each day is separated into four sections:

1. A Simple Thought

2. God's Word for You Today

3. A Moment to Reflect

4. An ocean image (photo, with comments to ponder)

Give yourself time to read "A Simple Thought" slowly. This thought will help your entry into the Scripture passage for the day. Each thought complements an image from the Hawaiian Islands. As you consider the image, you may find your mind wandering. Let it wander. God may be speaking to you as you think about His work in creation.

Next, take time to pray. Ask God to open your mind and give you the ability to hear Him speak to you through His Word. Each day you have been given a good chunk of Scripture. These scriptures were chosen intentionally to walk you through the entire story of God's relationship with humanity.

If you haven't read much of the Bible, these devotions will give you an overview of the Old and New Testaments. As you study these words written over a period of thousands of years, by a variety of writers, you will hear God's consistent message of love and protection.

Take some time to reflect on what you've read. Reflection questions will help you discover how God's Word can have an impact on your day. Consider keeping a journal as you answer these questions. At the end of this study, a journal can serve as a reminder of how your relationship with God has developed over the 40-day period.

Finally, enjoy the image for each day. After you have spent time in God's Word, slow down and listen to how God may speak to you through the image. Some days you may find that you simply like the photo; some days you may dwell with the image for a long time. Either way, these images have been specifically selected to help you hear and discover God's voice from the midst of creation.

- Tom Stephen & Virginia Starkey

God is seeking you. Does the thought that God is seeking you make you feel afraid or excited?

A Simple Thought

Do you remember a time when you felt vulnerable?

It can happen in an instant. You could be driving down the road, oblivious to danger, and suddenly someone slams into your car. *Life changes.*

Or you could receive a phone call from a friend who tells you that someone you love has been diagnosed with cancer. *Life changes.*

Or what about when you're having a great day in the surf with your friends, and suddenly a random set rolls in and you find yourself ducking under a massive amount of white water. *Life changes.*

Maybe you've always felt afraid. Deep inside, you wonder if you and those you love will be okay. Others talk about things "always working out," but in your quiet moments, you wonder if life will ever feel secure.

When God created the universe, He created a place in which everything we could ever want was provided. Adam and Eve had everything: food, water, companionship and a close relationship with God. God even walked with them in the garden on a regular basis, enjoying His creation.

When Adam and Eve chose to walk away from God, they became afraid. Life changed. It wasn't the way it was supposed to be. And it could never be the same for them again. That fear has plagued humanity ever since.

Before reading the Scripture passage below, pray that God would help you to understand who He is and who He created you to be.

God's Word for You Today: Genesis 3:1-10, *RSV*

··

Now the serpent was more subtle than any other wild creature that the LORD God had made. He said to the woman, "Did God say, 'You shall not eat of any tree of the garden'?"

And the woman said to the serpent, "We may eat of the fruit of the trees of the garden; but God said, 'You shall not eat of the fruit of the tree which is in the midst of the garden, neither shall you touch it, lest you die.' "

But the serpent said to the woman, "You will not die. For God knows that when you eat of it your eyes will be opened, and you will be like God, knowing good and evil."

So when the woman saw that the tree was good for food, and that it was a delight to the eyes, and that the tree was to be desired to make one wise, she took of its fruit and ate; and she also gave some to her husband, and he ate. Then the eyes of both were opened, and they knew that they were naked; and they sewed fig leaves together and made themselves aprons.

And they heard the sound of the LORD God walking in the garden in the cool of the day, and the man and his wife hid themselves from the presence of the LORD God among the trees of the garden. But the LORD God called to the man, and said to him, "Where are you?"

And he said, "I heard the sound of thee in the garden, and I was afraid, because I was naked; and I hid myself."

··

A Moment to Reflect

....

Can you remember when you first felt fear? When have you recently experienced fear?
Adam and Eve turned away from God because they wanted more. God had given them everything they needed,
but they wanted to be like God. Has there been a time when your desire for more caused you to turn away from
God's way of life?

....

FEAR BECOMES LAUGHTER   Day 2

A Simple Thought

At times it's difficult to believe that some circumstances will work out.

When you've hoped for something for years, and nothing happens, it's easy to give up. It's easy to become bitter and cynical.

We live in a world filled with people who have given up. And for good reason—their lives have not turned out as they had planned. When life puts our dreams on hold, fear prevents us from believing again.

In the Old Testament, we read that God promised Sarah and Abraham a child. They dreamed of raising a son. Despite their best efforts, 70 years passed, and they were still childless. Sarah gave up hoping for a child. The dream that God had spoken to them seemed like nothing more than a cruel joke.

(God's schedule rarely matches our expectations.)

Years after, Sarah chuckled to herself when God reminded Abraham of their promised child. But God knows our unspoken fears, and He speaks to our fear. Sarah met a God who makes all things possible.

Before reading the Scripture passage, pray that God will help you to understand who He is and who He created you to be.

This unknown surfer will be laughing at the end of this wave. Will you take a chance and trust God with your life today?

God's Word for You Today: Genesis 18:1-2,9-15

....

The LORD appeared to Abraham near the great trees of Mamre while he was sitting at the entrance to his tent in the heat of the day. Abraham looked up and saw three men standing nearby.

"Where is your wife Sarah?" they asked him. "There, in the tent," he said.

Then the LORD said, "I will surely return to you about this time next year, and Sarah your wife will have a son." Now Sarah was listening at the entrance to the tent, which was behind him. Abraham and Sarah were already old and well advanced in years, and Sarah was past the age of childbearing. So Sarah laughed to herself as she thought, "After I am worn out and my master is old, will I now have this pleasure?"

Then the LORD said to Abraham, "Why did Sarah laugh and say, 'Will I really have a child, now that I am old?' Is anything too hard for the LORD? I will return to you at the appointed time next year and Sarah will have a son."

Sarah was afraid, so she lied and said, "I did not laugh." But he said, "Yes, you did laugh."

....

A Moment to Reflect

....

What do you learn about God's character from this story of Sarah?

How does God give Sarah reason to hope? What hope do you have from reading this passage?

When Sarah discovered that God heard her laugh, she became afraid and lied. God understands the pain of

disappointment and the reality of doubt. Did God reject Sarah because of her fear? Will God reject you?

....

In the midst of darkness, God provides for those in need. Is this a sunset or sunrise? Can you find joy in both?

....

Fear is the path to the dark side. Fear leads to anger. Anger leads to hate. Hate leads to suffering.

- Yoda -

A Simple Thought

Fear causes nice people to act like idiots.

On a crowded day in the ocean, surfers become aggressive and agitated at each other. When a set rolls in, tensions rise as everyone scrambles for this limited resource. Instead of being thankful for the gift of a good day, people fight for what they believe should be theirs.

It's much like a group of shoppers on the day after Christmas who rudely disregard others in search of the best deal. Everyone's afraid someone else will get what they want.

Fortunately, God looks out for us even when others only look out for themselves.

Sarah found joy in a son. She quickly lost that joy because she was jealous of another son born to her husband. Her jealousy gave birth to fear. Her fear turned to anger. In anger she cast another mother and her son out into the desert.

Hagar and Ishmael, Abraham's other family, were abandoned by everyone. Hagar became a single parent with no child support. Ishmael no longer had a father. All was lost.

And then God showed up.

Before reading the Scripture passage, pray that God will help you to understand who He is and who He created you to be.

....

God's Word for You Today: Genesis 21:6-10,14-18, *RSV*

....

And Sarah said, "God has made laughter for me; every one who hears will laugh over me." And she said, "Who would have said to Abraham that Sarah would suckle children? Yet I have borne him a son in his old age."

And the child grew, and was weaned; and Abraham made a great feast on the day that Isaac was weaned. But Sarah saw the son of Hagar the Egyptian, whom she had borne to Abraham, playing with her son Isaac. So she said to Abraham, "Cast out this slave woman with her son; for the son of this slave woman shall not be heir with my son Isaac."

So Abraham rose early in the morning, and took bread and a skin of water, and gave it to Hagar, putting it on her shoulder, along with the child, and sent her away. And she departed, and wandered in the wilderness of Beersheba.

When the water in the skin was gone, she cast the child under one of the bushes. Then she went, and sat down over against him a good way off, about the distance of a bowshot; for she said, "Let me not look upon the death of the child." And as she sat over against him, the child lifted up his voice and wept.

And God heard the voice of the lad; and the angel of God called to Hagar from heaven, and said to her, "What troubles you, Hagar? Fear not; for God has heard the voice of the lad where he is. Arise, lift up the lad, and hold him fast with your hand; for I will make him a great nation."

....

A Moment to Reflect

Can you remember when you first felt fear? When have you recently experienced fear?

Can you think of a time when someone else's fear resulted in your pain?

Have you ever inflicted harm on someone because you were afraid of not getting what you wanted? What happened?

Her family rejected Hagar and Ishmael, but God did not abandon them. When have you been rejected by others? What do you think God would say to you?

If you know that you have hurt others because of your fear, take a moment to confess these actions to God and then resolve to seek the person you've offended. If you've been hurt by others, take time to cry out to God, asking for mercy on your situation.

What are your thoughts when you look at this photo about learning to fear and respect God's power? About listening to Him?

....

A Simple Thought

It's hard to try again when you've been burned one too many times in a relationship; you felt that God was calling you to pursue a ministry, but it didn't work out; your dream job becomes a nightmare.

When life doesn't go as expected, it's easy to give up.

Moses thought his purpose in life was to free a group of slaves from an evil king. He tried to organize a rebellion and killed a man, but none of the slaves were interested. Moses failed when he attempted to do the right thing.

Afterwards, Moses determined to never fail again, so he ran. He ran as far away as he could. He left God, and his people, and went to the desert.

Yet God never left Moses or gave up on him. God's purpose for Moses included leading the Hebrew slaves to freedom; but Moses had to learn to fear God. He had to learn how to follow God's plan instead of going his own way. God's ways are not our ways.

Just as a young surfer must learn to respect the power and unpredictability of the ocean in order to conquer his fear after a terrible wipeout, we must learn to respect God's power to mold us when we've sought to control our own destinies and failed.

Before reading the Scripture passage, pray that God will help you to understand who He is and who He created you to be.

....

God's Word for You Today: Exodus 3:1-6

Now Moses was tending the flock of Jethro his father-in-law, the priest of Midian, and he led the flock to the far side of the desert and came to Horeb, the mountain of God. There the angel of the LORD appeared to him in flames of fire from within a bush. Moses saw that though the bush was on fire it did not burn up. So Moses thought, "I will go over and see this strange sight—why the bush does not burn up."

When the LORD saw that he had gone over to look, God called to him from within the bush, "Moses! Moses!" And Moses said, "Here I am."

"Do not come any closer," God said. "Take off your sandals, for the place where you are standing is holy ground." Then he said, "I am the God of your father, the God of Abraham, the God of Isaac and the God of Jacob." At this, Moses hid his face, because he was afraid to look at God.

When have you sought to do something on your own, only to fail, and then you realized that God wanted to do it with you?

How would having a fear of God change the way you have experienced other fears in your life?

God shaped Moses in the desert to set him apart for a great purpose. Do you sense that God has a purpose for your life? Are you willing to humble yourself and ask God to reveal that purpose to you?

Today, as you spend time in prayer, remove your shoes, for God is with you. His presence makes this space holy. Spend time talking to God about your purpose and your fears.

Consider how your life would be different if you trusted God enough to live the way He is calling you to live. What step can you take to begin that life today?

FEAR OF THE UNKNOWN

....

A Simple Thought

We often fear what we don't know.

Even when change would be good for us, fear of an uncertain future paralyzes us from moving forward. We find it easier to do what is familiar rather than what would be best.

Friends and family may believe that our lives will be better if we change, but we're not so sure. Is it possible to trust God when you really don't see any good options?

In yesterday's Scripture, Moses learned to fear God. Fear turned to trust. After years of trusting God, Moses became a savior to a group of slaves, who were God's special possession.

But the people Moses freed did not know God. They saw Him work, and they knew about God, but they did not know God. While Moses saw a God of love and deliverance, the people only saw darkness and smoke. They didn't understand and were afraid. They considered that living in slavery might be a better option than placing their lives in the hands of this strange God.

The people kept their distance from God. After all, if they got too close, God might start to change things. And that was a frightening thought to them.

Before reading the Scripture passage, pray that God will help you to understand who He is and who He created you to be.

God's Word for You Today: Exodus 20:18-21

When the people saw the thunder and lightning and heard the trumpet and saw the mountain in smoke, they trembled with fear. They stayed at a distance and said to Moses, "Speak to us yourself and we will listen. But do not have God speak to us or we will die."

Moses said to the people, "Do not be afraid. God has come to test you, so that the fear of God will be with you to keep you from sinning."

The people remained at a distance, while Moses approached the thick darkness where God was.

A Moment to Reflect

Moses told the people, "Do not be afraid"; and then he said, "fear of God will keep you from sinning." What message was he trying to give the people? What message does God have for you in these words? What would you say is the difference between knowing about God and knowing God?

Have you ever stood alone when others just watched?
Ask God also to give you the ability to be the one voice who speaks for Him.

A Simple Thought

Sometimes we just don't get it.

Even though God assures us that we don't need to panic, we don't listen. Life's obstacles overwhelm our sense of security.

When life gets crazy, be careful to whom you listen. God will still speak, but the voice of the crowd can become overwhelming.

Although God freed the people of Israel from slavery and provided for their every need, the crowd saw too many obstacles when He called them to move into a new land. Instead of remembering God's faithfulness, they panicked. Giants inhabited the land He had given them. They thought that life with God in the new land would be easy. When it wasn't, they wanted to give up.

Apparently, even when you follow God, you will face some giant problems.

Much like a recovering alcoholic who sometimes feels called back to the slavery of drink after years of being clean, the voice of the crowd often beckons us to take the easy and destructive way out.

But there is another voice: Often in a crowd of fear, one or two voices will speak on God's behalf. To whom will we listen? Will we join in the amazing adventure that God has for us or will we sit on the sidelines and watch others experience the joy of life?

Before reading the Scripture passage, pray that God will help you to understand who He is and who He created you to be.

God's Word for You Today: Numbers 14:1-10

That night all the people of the community raised their voices and wept aloud. All the Israelites grumbled against Moses and Aaron, and the whole assembly said to them, "If only we had died in Egypt! Or in this desert! Why is the LORD bringing us to this land only to let us fall by the sword? Our wives and children will be taken as plunder. Wouldn't it be better for us to go back to Egypt?" And they said to each other, "We should choose a leader and go back to Egypt."

Then Moses and Aaron fell facedown in front of the whole Israelite assembly gathered there. Joshua son of Nun and Caleb son of Jephunneh, who were among those who had explored the land, tore their clothes and said to the entire Israelite assembly, "The land we passed through and explored is exceedingly good. If the LORD is pleased with us, he will lead us into that land, a land flowing with milk and honey, and will give it to us. Only do not rebel against the LORD. And do not be afraid of the people of the land, because we will swallow them up. Their protection is gone, but the LORD is with us. Do not be afraid of them."

But the whole assembly talked about stoning them.

A Moment to Reflect

....

Can you think of a time when fear stopped you from doing what you thought you could or should do?

Are you more easily influenced by the crowd or the voice calling you to trust God? Why?

Over the past month, how have you been tempted to "go back to Egypt" when God is calling you to go to the "promised land"?

....

Do you find peace or fear in a sunset? Do you need to fear those who are more powerful than you?

FEAR OF THE POWERFUL   Day 7

....

A Simple Thought

All people are equal in God's sight.

In yesterday's Scripture passage, the people of Israel were afraid to enter into the land God promised them. Because of their fear, God did not allow them to enter, but led them through the desert for 40 years.

Now, the next generation stands at the entrance to the new land. This time, they are ready to go in. They have learned from their parents' mistakes.

During the 40 years of wandering, God helped them to become a great nation. Unable to lead such a big group, Moses placed other leaders in charge. When there were problems, the new leaders could help make the decisions.

Yet Moses was concerned that human nature might cause these new leaders to give preference to the rich and powerful. When someone has power, it is easy to be afraid that they might execute that power if we go against their wishes.

Sometimes our fear can cause us to listen to the powerful more quickly than to the servant. The loudest or strongest voice should not lead or determine our actions, but rather the voice on the side of justice.

We can allow God to guide our decisions.

Before you read Moses' instructions for the leaders, pray that God will help you to understand who He is and who He created you to be.

....

God's Word for You Today: Deuteronomy 1:15-17

....

So I took the leading men of your tribes, wise and respected men, and appointed them to have authority over you—as commanders of thousands, of hundreds, of fifties and of tens and as tribal officials. And I charged your judges at that time: Hear the disputes between your brothers and judge fairly, whether the case is between brother Israelites or between one of them and an alien. Do not show partiality in judging; hear both small and great alike. Do not be afraid of any man, for judgment belongs to God.

....

A Moment to Reflect

....

Make a list of words that would complete this sentence, "I am intimidated by people who . . ."

As you listen to a friend's problems, or intervene with your children or lead others at work, do you give
preference to someone out of fear? How do the words "do not be afraid of any man" speak to that fear?

God gave the people of Israel trusted leaders to help them in times of indecision. The leaders helped to calm
the fears of those in need. Take a moment to list the people God has given you to help you in times of deci-
sion. Make a list of the people God has given you to calm your fears.

As you pray, ask God to still the voices of the crowd and open your heart to hear His message for you.

How have you been prepared for your next challenge?

FEAR OF A NEW CHALLENGE

....

A Simple Thought

Some of us never take on a new challenge, because we're afraid.

We're afraid of failure, afraid of not doing a perfect job, afraid of not being as good as other people doing the same thing, afraid of not having all the answers to possible problems in the future.

Things haven't changed much in the past 3,000 years. Joshua had the same fear. He was given the challenge of leading God's people when Moses died. Moses was such a great leader. How could anyone fill his shoes?

On his own, Joshua had reason to fear. But like Moses, God never intended for Joshua to lead on his own or have all the right answers. God would lead as Joshua followed. God's challenge to Joshua was: Will you follow Me? Joshua could face his new challenge on his own, or he could face his new adventure following the One who gave him the task.

St. Ignatius once said, "Work as if everything depends on God, and pray as if everything depends on you." In other words, when we know that God is in control, we have courage to face our next challenge.

Before reading the Scripture passage, pray that God will help you to understand who He is and who He created you to be.

....

God's Word for You Today: Joshua 1:1-9

··

After the death of Moses the servant of the LORD, the LORD said to Joshua son of Nun, Moses' aide: "Moses my servant is dead. Now then, you and all these people, get ready to cross the Jordan River into the land I am about to give to them—to the Israelites. I will give you every place where you set your foot, as I promised Moses. Your territory will extend from the desert to Lebanon, and from the great river, the Euphrates—all the Hittite country—to the Great Sea on the west. No one will be able to stand up against you all the days of your life. As I was with Moses, so I will be with you; I will never leave you nor forsake you.

"Be strong and courageous, because you will lead these people to inherit the land I swore to their forefathers to give them. Be strong and very courageous. Be careful to obey all the law my servant Moses gave you; do not turn from it to the right or to the left, that you may be successful wherever you go. Do not let this Book of the Law depart from your mouth; meditate on it day and night, so that you may be careful to do everything written in it. Then you will be prosperous and successful. Have I not commanded you? Be strong and courageous. Do not be terrified; do not be discouraged, for the LORD your God will be with you wherever you go."

··

{ A Moment to Reflect }

··

What is the biggest challenge facing you right now?

How does knowing that God is with you give you strength to face the challenge?

God instructed Joshua to find strength and wisdom by meditating on God's words. Read verse 9 again—which begins with the words, "Have I not commanded you?" and continue to the end.

Read this verse several times and reflect on how the words can have an impact on your life today.

Whatever fears you face today, God will be with you.

··

The reef holds the possibility of ripping this man apart, and yet he stands. Will you take a stand today?

....

A Simple Thought

When a huge swell hits the coast of Hawaii, many inexperienced surfers begin to talk big. They tell others how they will conquer the mountains of water that crash into the shore. The experienced surfers let their actions speak for themselves.

People with insecurities will often try to put on a show of strength to hide their fear. Those who live with fear will draw attention to themselves in the hope of convincing themselves and others that they can handle any situation.

One of the greatest men in Israel experienced deep insecurities. God told King Saul to do one thing, but Saul chose instead to do what the people wanted.

Saul chose to please people instead of God. He then experienced life without God. He thought that a quick offering of prayer and a promise to do better next time could make things right with God. God, however, wants us to take a stand for Him even in the midst of our fears. When we turn away from God, He won't force us to come back.

Fear may cause you to do things you never intended. But remember, you have a choice. Will you choose God?

Before you read what God said to Saul through His prophet Samuel, pray that God will help you to understand who He is and who He created you to be.

....

God's Word for You Today: 1 Samuel 15:22-30

....

And Samuel said, "Does the LORD delight in burnt offerings and sacrifices as much as in obeying the voice of the LORD? To obey is better than sacrifice, and to heed is better than the fat of rams. For rebellion is like the sin of divination, and arrogance like the evil of idolatry. Because you have rejected the word of the LORD, he has rejected you as king."

Then Saul said to Samuel, "I have sinned. I violated the LORD's command and your instructions. I was afraid of the people and so I gave in to them. Now I beg you, forgive my sin and come back with me, so that I may worship the LORD."

But Samuel said to him, "I will not go back with you. You have rejected the word of the LORD, and the LORD has rejected you as king over Israel!" As Samuel turned to leave, Saul caught hold of the hem of his robe, and it tore. Samuel said to him, "The LORD has torn the kingdom of Israel from you today and has given it to one of your neighbors—to one better than you. He who is the Glory of Israel does not lie or change his mind; for he is not a man, that he should change his mind."

Saul replied, "I have sinned. But please honor me before the elders of my people and before Israel; come back with me, so that I may worship the LORD your God." So Samuel went back with Saul, and Saul worshiped the LORD.

....

A Moment to Reflect

Consider a time in your life when your insecurities caused you to please other people instead of God. What was the result? Saul returned to the Lord even though he faced the consequences of his actions. Take a moment to pray and ask God to show you where your insecurities are causing you to turn away from Him.

A Simple Thought

"The task is just too big; I can't do it." "I don't have enough experience." "I'm not old enough." "It's just too hard."

All of us will face challenges that are simply too much for us to handle. We will find ourselves overwhelmed and discouraged even before we begin. Although we may try to have a positive outlook, deep down we know we're not prepared.

Often, those times are when we find that God has been preparing the situation for us instead of preparing us for the situation. He wants someone who will trust Him to do a great work. God does not necessarily call those who are equipped; He equips those He calls as they turn to Him.

As a young man, God called Solomon to be king and to build the Temple. Solomon did not know how to do construction. He did not know how to manage people. He was not prepared at all. But God was.

David, his father, gave Solomon some great advice.

Today, as you read what David told his son at the beginning of this huge project, pray that God will help you to understand who He is and who He created you to be.

Even though the man may feel alone in the air, he is still connected to the boat.
Will you stay connected to your source of strength—the Lord—today?

God's Word for You Today: 1 Chronicles 28:20-21

David also said to Solomon his son, "Be strong and courageous, and do the work. Do not be afraid or discouraged, for the LORD God, my God, is with you. He will not fail you or forsake you until all the work for the service of the temple of the LORD is finished. The divisions of the priests and Levites are ready for all the work on the temple of God, and every willing man skilled in any craft will help you in all the work. The officials and all the people will obey your every command."

A Moment to Reflect

Can you think of a time in which you found yourself in a situation for which you were totally unprepared? Perhaps you find yourself facing a challenge today that seems unmanageable. God may have prepared this situation for you to trust Him. Take time to meditate on these words and repeat them slowly as you consider how they can have an impact on your life today:

Be strong and courageous, and do the work. Do not be afraid or discouraged, for the LORD God, my God, is with you. He will not fail you or forsake you until all the work . . . is finished.

Spend time with God, speaking to Him about your day. And pray for others you know who are facing a difficult challenge. Take a moment sometime today to contact them and give them a word of encouragement.

Imagine seeing a wave runner flying over your head while you stood on this wave. Would you shrink in terror?

....

A Simple Thought

Even people of great faith, who live fearlessly, experience days of terror and discouragement. That's the problem with evil—it keeps coming back for more.

The cancer that had gone into remission returns with a vengeance.

The community that has finally recovered from a terrorist attack becomes a target once again.

You finally have financial security at your job when the company announces that it will begin downsizing soon.

After years of trying to have a baby, the pregnancy ends with a miscarriage in the eleventh week.

There are days when even the strongest get tired, discouraged and beaten down.

One of the greatest prophets in Israel, Elijah, experienced great fear after seeing God defeat his enemies. Elijah stood alone (with God) and defeated 400 of his enemies through prayer and faith. He thought the battle was over. The next day, when confronted by one woman—Jezebel, the queen of an evil empire—he ran away in fear and discouragement.

How did God respond to Elijah? The same way he responds to us in our fears: with His presence and the assurance that we are not alone. Elijah is given food and rest. Then God speaks.

Before reading how Elijah responded to God, pray that God will help you to understand who He is and who He created you to be.

....

God's Word for You Today: 1 Kings 19:1-18, *RSV*

Ahab told Jezebel all that Elijah had done, and how he had slain all the prophets with the sword. Then Jezebel sent a messenger to Elijah, saying, "So may the gods do to me, and more also, if I do not make your life as the life of one of them by this time tomorrow."

Then he was afraid, and he arose and went for his life, and came to Beersheba, which belongs to Judah, and left his servant there. But he himself went a day's journey into the wilderness, and came and sat down under a broom tree; and he asked that he might die, saying, "It is enough; now, O LORD, take away my life; for I am no better than my fathers."

And he lay down and slept under a broom tree; and behold, an angel touched him, and said to him, "Arise and eat." And he looked, and behold, there was at his head a cake baked on hot stones and a jar of water. And he ate and drank, and lay down again.

And the angel of the LORD came again a second time, and touched him, and said, "Arise and eat, else the journey will be too great for you." And he arose, and ate and drank, and went in the strength of that food forty days and forty nights to Horeb the mount of God. And there he came to a cave, and lodged there; and behold, the word of the LORD came to him, and he said to him, "What are you doing here, Elijah?"

He said, "I have been very jealous for the LORD, the God of hosts; for the people of Israel have forsaken thy covenant, thrown down thy altars, and slain thy prophets with the sword; and I, even I only, am left; and they seek my life, to take it away."

And he said, "Go forth, and stand upon the mount before the LORD." And behold, the LORD passed by, and a great and strong wind rent the mountains, and broke in pieces the rocks before the LORD, but the LORD was not in the wind; and after the wind an earthquake, but the LORD was not in the earthquake; and after the earthquake a fire, but the LORD was not in the fire; and after the fire a still small voice. And when Elijah heard it, he wrapped his face in his mantle and went out and stood at the entrance of the cave. And behold, there came a voice to him, and said, "What are you doing here, Elijah?"

He said, "I have been very jealous for the LORD, the God of hosts; for the people of Israel have forsaken thy covenant, thrown down thy altars, and slain thy prophets with the sword; and I, even I only, am left; and they seek my life, to take it away."

And the LORD said to him, "Go, return on your way to the wilderness of Damascus; and when you arrive, you shall anoint Hazael to be king over Syria; and Jehu the son of Nimshi you shall anoint to be king over Israel; and Elisha the son of Shaphat of Abel-meholah you shall anoint to be prophet in your place. And him who escapes from the sword of Hazael shall Jehu slay; and him who escapes from the sword of Jehu shall Elisha slay. Yet I will leave seven thousand in Israel, all the knees that have not bowed to Baal, and every mouth that has not kissed him."

Circumstances cause us to fear, and for good reason. Have you ever felt like the man in this image?

A Simple Thought

Have you ever faced a difficult situation completely alone? Has God ever seemingly abandoned you in a desperate circumstance?

Why would my parents divorce and not want to spend time with me?

How could God just watch when I was abused?

Why would God allow my friend to die in an unexpected accident?

When life deals a heavy blow, we often wonder why a loving God would leave us to face these things alone. Even when we discern some purpose from a terrible event, a question continues to nag at our hearts: Couldn't God do this good work without my having to suffer?

Since the beginning of time, we've been asking those questions. Faithful people who trust and love God have asked those questions. King David asked them back in the year A.D. 1000. Jesus asked them when He was on the cross and was brutally assaulted and killed. He felt the pain of God's absence. And God let Him die.

And then God brought life. Yes, God brought life, but He never removed the pain of His absence. Rather, He redeemed that pain.

As you read Psalm 22, consider what this passage tells you about God and about how faithful people respond to God in the midst of hardship.

God's Word for You Today: Psalm 22:1-5

....

My God, my God, why have you forsaken me? Why are you so far from saving me, so far from the words of my groaning?

O my God, I cry out by day, but you do not answer, by night, and am not silent.

Yet you are enthroned as the Holy One; you are the praise of Israel.

In you our fathers put their trust; they trusted and you delivered them.

They cried to you and were saved; in you they trusted and were not disappointed.

....

A Moment to Reflect

Have you ever simply poured out your heart to God? He knows your pain and your joy. Express to Him the fear or joy you feel today.

How does knowing that Jesus once felt abandoned by God affect how you might approach God when you are afraid? How does knowing that God brought Jesus back to life give you hope?

David, the writer of Psalm 22, acknowledges that God works in the lives of others, even when he doesn't feel God's presence. Reflect on how you have seen or heard about God working in the world around you. Spend some time talking honestly with God about your fears and frustrations.

God is with you at the beginning and ending of each day. Will you ask Him to watch over you today?

NO FEAR, GOD IS NEAR

....

A Simple Thought

A fearful child clings to his parents for protection. As children, we believe that our parents can keep us safe in all situations. As adults, we realize our vulnerability; and so we seek to protect ourselves from our fears using retirement accounts, home security systems, regular exercise, seatbelts and friendships.

Here's the problem: Stock markets crash, and we can lose our retirement; thieves can thwart the best security; people who exercise still suffer disease; seatbelts cannot control other drivers; and sometimes friends move away, or pass away.

We can lose our sense of security in an instant. Is there anyone or anything that we can fully trust?

Psalm 23 describes a God who cares for our every need: rest, food, security, even eternity. You have a Shepherd who protects and watches over you. If you've ever stood on the beach at sunset and felt the peace of the warm off-shore breezes, you understand what it means when the psalm talks about God leading us beside still waters.

God walks with us through the valley of the shadow of death. The shadow of death touches each of us, whether we face literal death or simply live a life that is dead to joy and love.

Before reading this psalm, pray that God will help you to understand who He is and who He created you to be.

God's Word for You Today: Psalm 23

The LORD is my shepherd, I shall not be in want.

He makes me lie down in green pastures, he leads me beside quiet waters, he restores my soul. He guides me in paths of righteousness for his name's sake.

Even though I walk through the valley of the shadow of death, I will fear no evil, for you are with me; your rod and your staff, they comfort me.

You prepare a table before me in the presence of my enemies. You anoint my head with oil; my cup overflows.

Surely goodness and love will follow me all the days of my life, and I will dwell in the house of the LORD forever.

God will protect and guide your day. Take a moment to ask Him to keep you aware of His presence throughout the day. Reflect on a time when you felt like you were walking through the valley of the shadow of death. How did knowing that God was with you bring you comfort? If you didn't know God at that time, how would a relationship with Him have made a difference in your fear?

Do you have people in your life who feel like enemies? Pray that God would encounter them today.

Did he make it? We don't know. We do know that he didn't hold back. How does this image encourage you to live with a heart full of praise?

A Simple Thought

In today's world, suicide bombers generate a subconscious fear in people. Even when we're having a normal day, underneath it all we've become aware that devastation from terrorists could happen anywhere at almost any time.

When vulnerability motivates people to isolate themselves and fail to live life fully, the terrorist experiences victory.

How can we respond to our fear? Praise.

Just as a person who is facing an assailant would jump with joy inside when a strong friend shows up, we can jump with joy knowing that God never abandons us.

We can face fear as we begin to praise God for His faithfulness to conquer those who seek to do us harm. In Psalm 56, David does not praise God for his difficult situation; rather, he praises God for His promise to carry him through his circumstance.

David's hope relies on the fact that God brings light in a dark situation. You have the same hope.

In fact, God does some of His best work in dark and chaotic situations.

Before reading the Scripture passage, pray that God would help you to understand who He is and who He created you to be.

God's Word for You Today: Psalm 56:1-4,10-13

....

Be merciful to me, O God, for men hotly pursue me; all day long they press their attack.

My slanderers pursue me all day long; many are attacking me in their pride.

When I am afraid, I will trust in you.

In God, whose word I praise, in God I trust; I will not be afraid. What can mortal man do to me?

In God, whose word I praise, in the LORD, whose word I praise—

in God I trust; I will not be afraid. What can man do to me?

I am under vows to you, O God; I will present my thank offerings to you.

For you have delivered me from death and my feet from stumbling, that I may walk before God in the light of life.

....

A Moment to Reflect

David learned to trust God. As a young shepherd boy protecting his father's sheep, he encountered lions and bears, and God used His strength to deliver him from harm. Have you ever experienced God's protection? How do your past experiences with God influence how you trust Him today?

As you consider the words of Psalm 56 a second time, choose a phrase that you would like to remember. Write it down in a place where you will be reminded to consider it throughout the day.

As you pray, mull over the times in your life when you have seen God's love, and thank Him for His protection.

As the day ends, you have an opportunity to start over.
How does this image help you see the possibilities of God doing something new?

NOT AFRAID TO TURN AROUND

A Simple Thought

Have you ever experienced the consequences of a bad decision?

Most of us have. We didn't study for a test, and so we failed it. We entertained the flirting of a coworker and found ourselves in an affair and eventually a divorce. We responded negatively to a client and lost an important account. We chose to turn away from God and found ourselves in a grave situation.

Many times we receive subtle warnings that we're making a bad decision, but we ignore them, thinking that everything will be alright. God sent warnings to His people thousands of years ago through messengers, and He sends warnings to us today.

Isaiah, God's messenger, realized that his people had turned away from God and placed their hope in political alliances and other gods. As a result, they lived in fear and in the certainty of destruction. They thought they could handle it, but without God, they soon found that their bad situation grew worse.

When we turn away from living as God intends, we experience a life that God never intended for us—one of desperation, fear and uncertainty.

Although we may turn away from living as God intends, God never turns His back on us. Rather, God loves us, forgives us and draws us back into a place of certainty and no fear. We once again are faced with a choice: Will we turn back and receive God's love, or face His judgment?

Pray that God would speak to you as you reflect on the words of hope that Isaiah gave to the people of Israel who were facing negative consequences for their actions.

God's Word for You Today: Isaiah 12:1-4

....

In that day you will say: "I will praise you, O LORD. Although you were angry with me, your anger has turned away and you have comforted me. Surely God is my salvation; I will trust and not be afraid. The LORD, the LORD, is my strength and my song; he has become my salvation." With joy you will draw water from the wells of salvation.

    In that day you will say: "Give thanks to the LORD, call on his name; make known among the nations what he has done, and proclaim that his name is exalted."

....

A Moment to Reflect

Is there a part of your life that you know God wants you to change but you have been resistant to change? How has that decision had a negative impact on your life?

Are you willing to follow God today and trust Him in every area of your life? Reflect on what your life would look like if the Lord was your strength and salvation.

Receive God's comfort today as you pray the words of this passage out loud. After speaking each phrase to God, tell Him how those words will affect your life today.

When we turn away from God, it can feel like a free fall. Have you turned away from God recently?

NO FEAR IN BELONGING

A Simple Thought

Nothing you do will cause God to love you more. Nothing you do will cause God to love you less. God desires that your life is good, full and satisfying. But you can choose an empty, dry life. If you choose to walk away from God, He won't force you to stay. He will allow your decisions to have their full effect.

- If you choose not to forgive, you will eventually become bitter.

- If you choose to continually pursue money, your life will be empty of meaning.

- If you choose to use others, you will experience loneliness.

- If you choose to walk away from God, you will live a life of insecurity.

The people of Israel felt abandoned by God. In reality, they bailed on Him. God offered them protection, but they chose to protect themselves so that they could pursue what they thought would bring them happiness.

Many of these people felt that God would never welcome them back. After all, they had their chance, and they rejected God. But even though they had given up on God, He never gave up on them.

You see, God chose the people of Israel to be His children. They belonged to Him. But just like a teenager who has broken his or her parents' trust one too many times, sometimes we don't feel like God will ever really forgive or trust us again.

Most of us don't feel worthy to approach God. And we're not. The good thing is that God doesn't look for a perfect person; He looks for a humble heart.

Read about how God responded to people who were afraid He would never welcome them back.

God's Word for You Today: Isaiah 44:1-5

....

But now listen, O Jacob, my servant, Israel, whom I have chosen.

    This is what the LORD says—he who made you, who formed you in the womb, and who will help you: Do not be afraid, O Jacob, my servant, Jeshurun, whom I have chosen.

    For I will pour water on the thirsty land, and streams on the dry ground; I will pour out my Spirit on your offspring, and my blessing on your descendants.

    They will spring up like grass in a meadow, like poplar trees by flowing streams.

    One will say, "I belong to the LORD"; another will call himself by the name of Jacob; still another will write on his hand, "The LORD's," and will take the name Israel.

....

A Moment to Reflect

....

How do these scriptural words of belonging address your fears that God will reject you for the choices you have made? God created you in the womb. He predestined you to know His love. Will you choose Him today?

Do you have any relationships that have suffered because of choices you have made? Are you afraid that you have lost those relationships forever? As you seek God's love and forgiveness, He will create in you the ability to love others. Place your fears of broken relationships in God's hand today.

....

This man doesn't place his focus on where he has been, but rather on where he is going.
Will you allow God to point you in the right direction today?

NO FEAR OF ATTACK
A Simple Thought

People often stress out over a situation before they have an actual problem. Most of us have a tendency to cultivate fear by worrying about what could happen instead of confronting the actual problem. The media, our friends, and even our own minds invite us to consider all the possible negative outcomes of a situation, and we become overwhelmed and afraid.

When faced with a difficult situation, even well-intentioned friends can create fear by speaking when they don't have all the facts.

Rumors and hearsay have plagued humanity for centuries. When foreign invaders ransacked the nation of Israel, the Jews were taken into captivity. Many of the Israelites believed that God had lost control and had abandoned them.

When the situation grew desperate, God's messenger Jeremiah spoke a word of truth. He proclaimed that the enemy, Babylon, would not have the last word. God would conquer their fears by conquering their enemies.

God continues this work today. As we face enemies such as disease, poverty, and even death, God speaks a word of truth to us. We have no need to fear, because He is powerful and near.

Before reading the Scripture passage, pray that God will help you to understand who He is and who He created you to be.

God's Word for You Today: Jeremiah 51:45-48

....

"Come out of her, my people! Run for your lives! Run from the fierce anger of the LORD.

Do not lose heart or be afraid when rumors are heard in the land; one rumor comes this year, another the next, rumors of violence in the land and of ruler against ruler.

For the time will surely come when I will punish the idols of Babylon; her whole land will be disgraced and her slain will all lie fallen within her.

Then heaven and earth and all that is in them will shout for joy over Babylon, for out of the north destroyers will attack her," declares the LORD.

....

A Moment to Reflect

....

What rumors or half-truths have caused you to live in fear?

Consider how you help others live with or without fear. What do you do? Do you offer words of hope, or do you help to create fear? How does this Scripture passage speak to your fears?

As you pray, consider the truth of the passage that God has power to do the impossible. God also has power to give you strength through an impossible situation.

How is God speaking to you today?

....

Consider the speed, the direction of the board and the size of this wave.
What would happen if this man hesitated at this moment?

*Fear causes hesitation and hesitation causes
your worst fears to come true.*
- Brody, from the movie *Point Break* -

A Simple Thought

Caution helps us to consider a safe alternative to a potentially dangerous situation. Yet at the point of decision, hesitation delivers disastrous results.

If you've chosen to follow God, you live in a potentially dangerous situation. Others will not always like the choices you've made, because your choices will cause them to think about their own relationship with God. When you're confronted by those who will challenge your decisions to live faithfully, will you hesitate and bow down to their fears, or will you trust God?

Daniel prayed constantly and lived a life that honored God and cared for people. When God blessed him with security and a lack of fear, others became jealous and sought to take his life. When faced with a choice between saving his life and following God, Daniel did not hesitate.

Even when he was afraid, he chose to trust God in a very difficult circumstance.

Before reading the Scripture passage, pray that God will help you to understand who He is and who He created you to be.

....

Then this Daniel became distinguished above all the other presidents and satraps, because an excellent spirit was in him; and the king planned to set him over the whole kingdom. Then the presidents and the satraps sought to find a ground for complaint against Daniel with regard to the kingdom; but they could find no ground for complaint or any fault, because he was faithful, and no error or fault was found in him. Then these men said, "We shall not find any ground for complaint against this Daniel unless we find it in connection with the law of his God."

Then these presidents and satraps came by agreement to the king and said to him, "O King Darius, live for ever! All the presidents of the kingdom, the prefects and the satraps, the counselors and the governors are agreed that the king should establish an ordinance and enforce an interdict, that whoever makes petition to any god or man for thirty days, except to you, O king, shall be cast into the den of lions. Now, O king, establish the interdict and sign the document, so that it cannot be changed, according to the law of the Medes and the Persians, which cannot be revoked." Therefore King Darius signed the document and interdict.

When Daniel knew that the document had been signed, he went to his house where he had windows in his upper chamber open toward Jerusalem; and he got down upon his knees three times a day and prayed and gave thanks before his God, as he had done previously.

Then the king commanded, and Daniel was brought and cast into the den of lions. The king said to Daniel, "May your God, whom you serve continually, deliver you!"

And a stone was brought and laid upon the mouth of the den, and the king sealed it with his own signet and with the signet of his lords, that nothing might be changed concerning Daniel. Then the king went to his palace, and spent the night fasting; no diversions were brought to him, and sleep fled from him.

Then, at break of day, the king arose and went in haste to the den of lions. When he came near to the den where Daniel was, he cried out in a tone of anguish and said to Daniel, "O Daniel, servant of the living God, has your God, whom you serve continually, been able to deliver you from the lions?"

Then Daniel said to the king, "O king, live for ever! My God sent his angel and shut the lions' mouths, and they have not hurt me, because I was found blameless before him; and also before you, O king, I have done no wrong."

Then the king was exceedingly glad, and commanded that Daniel be taken up out of the den. So Daniel was taken up out of the den, and no kind of hurt was found upon him, because he had trusted in his God.

....

Meditate on the image of the rainbow over this desolate land.
How has God provided for creation in the midst of natural disasters?

A Simple Thought

Early on the morning of Sunday, December 26, 2004, a massive earthquake measuring 9.0 on the Richter scale occurred in the Indian Ocean. The original quake triggered powerful tsunamis that devastated the coastal areas of India, Indonesia, Sri Lanka, Thailand, Maldives and other islands in the area. More than 150,000 people were killed, making it one of the deadliest disasters in modern history.

The loss of life, of natural habitats and the feeling of security from this disaster cannot be measured. How does one live securely in a world in which this can happen?

Natural disasters have plagued people since the beginning of time. One of God's messengers, Joel, received a command from God to speak words of comfort to people who lived through a natural disaster—an invasion of locusts had decimated the land. People wondered if they would ever recover.

Natural disasters exist as a part of our world. God, however, provides before, during and after such events. As you read the Scripture from the book of Joel, consider what these words say about God and His work in the world.

God's Word for You Today: Joel 2:21-26

....

Be not afraid, O land; be glad and rejoice. Surely the LORD has done great things. Be not afraid, O wild animals, for the open pastures are becoming green. The trees are bearing their fruit; the fig tree and the vine yield their riches.

Be glad, O people of Zion, rejoice in the LORD your God, for he has given you the autumn rains in righteousness. He sends you abundant showers, both autumn and spring rains, as before.

The threshing floors will be filled with grain; the vats will overflow with new wine and oil.

"I will repay you for the years the locusts have eaten—the great locust and the young locust, the other locusts and the locust swarm—my great army that I sent among you.

You will have plenty to eat, until you are full, and you will praise the name of the LORD your God, who has worked wonders for you; never again will my people be shamed."

....

A Moment to Reflect

How would you describe the character of God, knowing that He provides for those who have been subject to a natural disaster?

How would these words strike you if you were the person suffering through a natural disaster?

What does it mean to have a healthy respect or fear of nature? What about respect or fear of God?

Take some time to pray for those who have suffered through a natural disaster. Ask God to grant you wisdom as to how God may use you to care for those in need.

Sometimes we are objects of wrath and sometimes we are objects of blessing. Which person do you most relate to in this image?

A Simple Thought

If your daughter had leukemia, would you allow her to suffer through the pain of chemotherapy and a bone-marrow transplant in order to remove the cancer?

What would you say when she asked, "Why do you let the doctors put me through so much pain?"

Sometimes we have to undergo temporary pain and suffering in order to become healthy. Although we may fear the pain in the moment, we know that the end result will be good.

The people of Israel suffered from a spiritual cancer for a long time. Their own greed, lust and desires caused them to turn away from God. The treatment for their cancer involved exile in the land of Babylon. They experienced the pain and fear of being outside of God's care and protection. Life became uncertain. The treatment worked. Because God judged them and allowed their lives to fall apart, they realized their need for God.

In the book of Zechariah, God responded to these people who had turned away from Him and were now ready to return by relieving their fear and welcoming them back, and telling them how to live a "cancer-free" life. Before reading the Scripture passage, pray that God will help you to understand who He is and who He created you to be.

God's Word for You Today: Zechariah 8:12-17

....

"The seed will grow well, the vine will yield its fruit, the ground will produce its crops, and the heavens will drop their dew. I will give all these things as an inheritance to the remnant of this people. As you have been an object of cursing among the nations, O Judah and Israel, so will I save you, and you will be a blessing. Do not be afraid, but let your hands be strong."

This is what the LORD Almighty says: "Just as I had determined to bring disaster upon you and showed no pity when your fathers angered me," says the LORD Almighty, "so now I have determined to do good again to Jerusalem and Judah. Do not be afraid. These are the things you are to do: Speak the truth to each other, and render true and sound judgment in your courts; do not plot evil against your neighbor, and do not love to swear falsely. I hate all this," declares the LORD.

....

A Moment to Reflect

This passage reveals a judgmental and compassionate God. In what ways have some decisions you've made brought consequences and judgment to your life? Are you tired of paying the price for those past mistakes?

How do the words of this passage bring you hope that God does forgive and welcome us back?

God calls the people to "not be afraid," and then He calls them to action: to speak the truth and not do evil. In what ways has God called you to love others and speak the truth today?

As you pray, confess any mistakes or actions you've made that have caused you to turn away from God so that you can receive His love and forgiveness today.

Sometimes life can feel very uncertain. What feelings does this image provoke in you?

FEAR OF UNCERTAINTY

....

A Simple Thought

As we leave behind our fears and begin to trust that God is near, our prayers will change. We move from, "Lord, be with me as I *make* my plans," to "Lord, make my plans and I will follow." We no longer simply ask for God's blessing; rather, we ask for His direction.

When life feels uncertain, it is harder to let God lead us. When He asks us to follow Him, we will often retreat in fear. We feel safer when we're in control.

As a young man, Joseph faithfully followed God. He planned to marry a beautiful young woman named Mary and eventually have children. Life was good. Life was planned. God's plan seemed predictable.

Having never slept with Mary, his fiancée, her announcement that she was carrying a child devastated his world. Joseph's plans were thrown into chaos. Fear and uncertainty prevailed as he furiously sought a solution. He determined to quietly leave Mary and start over.

But God had different plans. Would Joseph follow God's plan into a life of uncertainty, or would he go his own way?

God often asks us to give up what we think is best for our lives to receive instead a life that He has planned for us—one that is better than we could imagine. The question is, Will we follow?

Before reading the Scripture passage, pray that God will help you to understand who He is and who He created you to be.

God's Word for You Today: Matthew 1:18-21

....

This is how the birth of Jesus Christ came about: His mother Mary was pledged to be married to Joseph, but before they came together, she was found to be with child through the Holy Spirit. Because Joseph her husband was a righteous man and did not want to expose her to public disgrace, he had in mind to divorce her quietly.

But after he had considered this, an angel of the Lord appeared to him in a dream and said, "Joseph son of David, do not be afraid to take Mary home as your wife, because what is conceived in her is from the Holy Spirit. She will give birth to a son, and you are to give him the name Jesus, because he will save his people from their sins."

A Moment to Reflect

Imagine if Joseph would have said no to God and left Mary. What do you think would have happened to his life? What about Mary's?

Has God called you to a plan that doesn't seem to match what you wanted or expected? Take a moment to consider again what God said to Joseph. What do you think God would say to you?

Joseph found answers as he spent time listening to God. God will also give you direction today as you talk honestly with Him about your life and plans. Pray.

We often feel tiny when we are afraid. Imagine God's hand guiding this man.

A Simple Thought

Peer pressure knows no age limit.

Some think that only teenagers bow down to others. But friends, the media, our culture and a variety of other voices influence each of us. People have power over us. Some have more power than others.

- Will you always do what the boss says because you're afraid of losing your job?
- Will you always follow your parents because you're afraid of disappointing them?
- Will you always do what your spouse says?
- Will you always do what feels right in the moment, even if you know it will be harmful in the long run?

Jesus makes the decision pretty simple: Let the One who loves you the most and who has the power to protect you have the greatest influence.

When you decide to follow God, it comes at a cost. When you decide to live differently from those around you, people may give you a hard time. You will always have a choice: Will you listen to God, or will you listen to others?

The real question is, Who do you fear?

Before reading the Scripture passage, pray that God would help you to understand who He is and who He created you to be.

God's Word for You Today: Matthew 10:26-31

So do not be afraid of them. There is nothing concealed that will not be disclosed, or hidden that will not be made known. What I tell you in the dark, speak in the daylight; what is whispered in your ear, proclaim from the roofs. Do not be afraid of those who kill the body but cannot kill the soul. Rather, be afraid of the One who can destroy both soul and body in hell. Are not two sparrows sold for a penny? Yet not one of them will fall to the ground apart from the will of your Father. And even the very hairs of your head are all numbered. So don't be afraid; you are worth more than many sparrows.

A Moment to Reflect

. . . .

When you were a child, what people had control over your life? Did you fear them or love them?

What fears influence how you live today? How do you want to live?

As you consider the words of Jesus one more time, what message do you sense God giving you today?

As you pray, tell God about your fears and listen to His words concerning those fears.

. . . .

Everybody starts small. How does the image of this man help you to understand that even small faith can have a great impact?

FEAR THAT YOU DON'T HAVE ENOUGH FAITH   Day 23

A Simple Thought

God's influence in our lives usually begins in a small way.

- A quiet voice of assurance to our hearts and minds when we're suffering.

- A word of comfort from a friend.

- A song on the radio, or words on a bumper sticker.

God's influence in our lives usually begins with something simple and then, if allowed to grow, increases to a tremendous influence on us and others.

As a culture, we've lost the discipline of starting small and nurturing slow, steady growth. In our instant "super-size me" culture, we want it all, and we want it now. If we don't have it today, somehow we fear that we'll miss out or not have enough.

Even when it comes to faith, we want to trust God completely—now! We think that we should be able to move mountains and raise people from the dead, when God simply wants us to start by saying "Thank you" and not taking our lives for granted.

Just as a small stone's ripple impacts the entire lake, a simple, small faith can influence the world.

As you read these parables of Jesus, pray that God will help you to understand who He is and who He created you to be.

God's Word for You Today: Matthew 13:31-33

....

He told them another parable: "The kingdom of heaven is like a mustard seed, which a man took and planted in his field. Though it is the smallest of all your seeds, yet when it grows, it is the largest of garden plants and becomes a tree, so that the birds of the air come and perch in its branches."

He told them still another parable: "The kingdom of heaven is like yeast that a woman took and mixed into a large amount of flour until it worked all through the dough."

....

A Moment to Reflect

....

Do you ever worry that you simply don't have enough faith to have a positive influence in the world? What impression did you receive from these parables of Jesus?

The farmer nurtures the mustard seed with water. The yeast affects the dough with heat. Our faith grows as we pray. Speak to God about the areas of your life in which you would like your faith to develop.

Do you know others who long to have the comfort that comes with knowing that God is with us? God may be calling you, with your little faith, to love and care for those who are hurting. Speak to Him on behalf of those you know.

....

When has an unexpected event turned your world upside down?

KEEPING YOUR FOCUS

A Simple Thought

Many of us have been living a lie.

Perhaps our parents taught us this lie, or maybe we heard it from our friends or the media; but for some reason, we've come to believe that if we work hard, if we're nice to our neighbors and we pay our taxes, life should be mostly trouble-free.

Sure, we'll have little frustrations, but none of us deserves to suffer. After all, if we follow God and are "good" people, shouldn't God protect us from the storms of life?

The problem is that storms come, and we're all vulnerable.

The disciples were simply following Jesus' command. Get into the boat and go across the lake. Who would have thought that going across the lake meant risking their lives? When a huge storm blew in, they were afraid.

Suddenly, a voice rumbled through the storm: "Take courage. It is I. Don't be afraid." Jesus did not remove the storm; rather, He entered it.

As you read this story of Jesus and His disciples, pray that God would help you to understand who He is and who He created you to be.

God's Word for You Today: Matthew 14:22-33

....

Immediately Jesus made the disciples get into the boat and go on ahead of him to the other side, while he dismissed the crowd. After he had dismissed them, he went up on a mountainside by himself to pray. When evening came, he was there alone, but the boat was already a considerable distance from land, buffeted by the waves because the wind was against it.

During the fourth watch of the night Jesus went out to them, walking on the lake. When the disciples saw him walking on the lake, they were terrified. "It's a ghost," they said, and cried out in fear.

But Jesus immediately said to them: "Take courage! It is I. Don't be afraid."

"Lord, if it's you," Peter replied, "tell me to come to you on the water."

"Come," he said.

Then Peter got down out of the boat, walked on the water and came toward Jesus. But when he saw the wind, he was afraid and, beginning to sink, cried out, "Lord, save me!"

Immediately Jesus reached out his hand and caught him. "You of little faith," he said, "why did you doubt?" And when they climbed into the boat, the wind died down. Then those who were in the boat worshiped him, saying, "Truly you are the Son of God."

....

A Moment to Reflect

....

What part of this story on the lake speaks to you? What do you sense God is teaching you?

Take a couple of minutes to meditate on these words of Jesus: "Take courage. It is I. Do not be afraid."

Peter's "little faith" allowed him to walk on water. Sure, he lost his focus for a while, but even then he called out to God for help. Are your eyes on Jesus today? Speak to Him about your "storm."

....

A Simple Thought

I suppose it would depend on what was happening at the time, but if God walked into a room where you were, would you feel afraid or enthralled?

If you were in prayer, you might welcome God with excitement. But if your words were hurting a loved one, or you were in the midst of another sin, you might cower in fear or embarrassment.

The presence of God brings light to dark situations. But just like physical light, we welcome it when we're afraid and avoid it when we want to keep certain things hidden.

The day Jesus died, some people were grateful to get rid of a problem, and others wept at the loss of a powerful friend. Neither group understood His death.

The first people to see Jesus after He rose from the dead were those guarding His tomb. When Jesus appeared in a great light, the soldiers cowered in fear.

Next, a group of women saw Jesus. They came to the tomb expecting to simply see His dead body; instead they found Him alive. Joy quickly replaced their fear.

If God were to come to you today, would you fear Him or welcome Him with joy?

As you read this story of Jesus, pray that God will help you to understand who He is and who He created you to be.

This image has both shadow and light. Do you see hope or fear in this image?
As you pray, do you desire to know God, or do you want to hide?

God's Word for You Today: Matthew 28:2-10

....

There was a violent earthquake, for an angel of the Lord came down from heaven and, going to the tomb, rolled back the stone and sat on it. His appearance was like lightning, and his clothes were white as snow. The guards were so afraid of him that they shook and became like dead men.

The angel said to the women, "Do not be afraid, for I know that you are looking for Jesus, who was crucified. He is not here; he has risen, just as he said. Come and see the place where he lay. Then go quickly and tell his disciples: 'He has risen from the dead and is going ahead of you into Galilee. There you will see him.' Now I have told you."

So the women hurried away from the tomb, afraid yet filled with joy, and ran to tell his disciples. Suddenly Jesus met them. "Greetings," he said. They came to him, clasped his feet and worshiped him. Then Jesus said to them, "Do not be afraid. Go and tell my brothers to go to Galilee; there they will see me."

....

A Moment to Reflect

....

If you don't know God, seeing Him can create fear. Have you ever felt the fear of God's presence?

Reflect on what brings fear and joy in seeing God.

Why would Jesus tell them, "Do not be afraid"? How do those words speak to you?

When the women saw Jesus, they worshiped Him. God is with you right now. Take time to worship Him.

....

This man has nowhere to go—the white water will swallow him up in seconds. Do you call on God in desperate situations?

A Simple Thought

When you need help, how long does it take you to admit it?

Many married couples will only seek counseling when the situation appears hopeless.

Many students will seek a tutor only after they've received a failing grade.

Some folks will not go to the doctor when they suffer a small amount of pain, only to find out later that a major problem could have been avoided if they had asked for help sooner.

We may pray for others, but we rarely pray for ourselves. After all, we can handle our problems. We don't want to bother God with our lives—that is, until things become unmanageable and fear sets in.

The crowd says, "You should have come in when you first felt a distancing from your husband; now it's too late to avoid divorce."

The crowd says, "If you had come in sooner, you would not have had to fail this class; now it's too late."

The crowd says, "If you had seen a doctor sooner, maybe we could have done something. Now it's too late to help you."

As you read the Scripture passage, pay attention to how Jesus treats a man who waited to come to Him until his daughter was near death. How does Jesus treat the crowd and their opinion of the man's situation?

God's Word for You Today: Mark 5:35-43

....

While Jesus was still speaking, some men came from the house of Jairus, the synagogue ruler. "Your daughter is dead," they said. "Why bother the teacher any more?"

Ignoring what they said, Jesus told the synagogue ruler, "Don't be afraid; just believe."

He did not let anyone follow him except Peter, James and John—the brother of James. When they came to the home of the synagogue ruler, Jesus saw a commotion, with people crying and wailing loudly. He went in and said to them, "Why all this commotion and wailing? The child is not dead but asleep." But they laughed at him.

After he put them all out, he took the child's father and mother and the disciples who were with him, and went in where the child was. He took her by the hand and said to her, "Talitha koum!" (which means, "Little girl, I say to you, get up!"). Immediately the girl stood up and walked around (she was twelve years old). At this they were completely astonished. He gave strict orders not to let anyone know about this, and told them to give her something to eat.

....

A Moment to Reflect

How do you think the man received Jesus' words, "Don't be afraid; just believe"?

Jesus calls us to listen to His voice of assurance and hope even when others tell us to give up. What situation in your life seems impossible? Go to Jesus now and talk with Him; tell Him about your life.

Just as Jesus took His disciples with Him to heal the girl, perhaps Jesus is calling you to go out and give His love to someone. Ask God to show you how to reach out to someone else today.

God often invites us into His plans that are already in motion.
Do you ever feel like you've been dropped into a new and unexpected plan?

A Simple Thought

Sometimes we pray out of habit, not really expecting God to do anything. Prayer becomes a way for us to express our thoughts and feelings in a quiet moment.

Expressing thoughts and feelings may help us feel better, but prayer is not simply a divine therapy session. In prayer, the God of creation gives us direction. Be careful though, because God may lead you in surprising ways. When God calls you to a new adventure, those routine prayers can be filled with questions and fear.

When Jesus Christ came to Earth, God called many people to be obedient. God called Zechariah, an old man with no children, to have a child with his barren wife. God called Mary to become an unwed pregnant teenager, carrying God's Son. (That's one adventure Mary could have never anticipated.)

God surprised Zechariah by answering a prayer that had become a habit. God surprised Mary by answering a prayer for the world that she had never uttered.

As you read these two stories, pray that God will help you to understand who He is and who He created you to be.

God's Word for You Today: Luke 1:11-13,18,29-35

....

Then an angel of the Lord appeared to him, standing at the right side of the altar of incense. When Zechariah saw him, he was startled and was gripped with fear. But the angel said to him: "Do not be afraid, Zechariah; your prayer has been heard. Your wife Elizabeth will bear you a son, and you are to give him the name John."

Zechariah asked the angel, "How can I be sure of this? I am an old man and my wife is well along in years."

Mary was greatly troubled at his words and wondered what kind of greeting this might be. But the angel said to her, "Do not be afraid, Mary, you have found favor with God. You will be with child and give birth to a son, and you are to give him the name Jesus. He will be great and will be called the Son of the Most High. The Lord God will give him the throne of his father David, and he will reign over the house of Jacob forever; his kingdom will never end."

"How will this be," Mary asked the angel, "since I am a virgin?"

The angel answered, "The Holy Spirit will come upon you, and the power of the Most High will overshadow you. So the holy one to be born will be called the Son of God."

....

A Moment to Reflect

The angel said, "Do not be afraid" to Zechariah because his routine prayers had been answered. If God answered your prayers, would you be shocked? How do the words "Do not be afraid" encourage you to keep praying over a long period of time? Have you given up on your prayers ever being answered?

The angel said, "Do not be afraid" to Mary because she had found favor with God. God saw something in Mary that gave her the ability to carry His Son. What does God see in you? Sit quietly and listen for God's voice, and ask Him to help you see yourself as He sees you.

If God were to appear to you, would you ask questions about God's ability to work or simply ask questions of what you are to do next?

God is with you. You have no need to fear. Follow Him today.

Sometimes God gives us more than we could ever imagine. Has God ever answered your prayers in a huge way?

A Simple Thought

Following God sometimes becomes so routine that we don't expect Him to do anything too radical. We go to church each Sunday. We try to serve our community. We're nice to our neighbors.

We believe that it's possible for God to do anything, but we don't really expect that He will. Perhaps it's habit, maybe pride, or maybe even a little bit of unbelief, but we live most of our lives thinking that we have God figured out.

And then, God does something so unexpected that we realize how much we've taken Him for granted:

· God spares your life with a miracle when everyone expected you to die.

· God gives you the money you need to cover your expenses.

· God blesses you with a boyfriend or girlfriend after years of thinking you would never find the

right person.

When God gives us more than we ever expected or wanted, we're afraid that He will discover that we really didn't believe. We're afraid that God may find our hidden sin of pride or unbelief. When that happens, God responds by telling us to not be afraid.

As you read this story of Jesus, pray that God will help you to understand who He is and who He created you to be.

God's Word for You Today: Luke 5:4-11

....

When he had finished speaking, he said to Simon, "Put out into deep water, and let down the nets for a catch."

Simon answered, "Master, we've worked hard all night and haven't caught anything. But because you say so, I will let down the nets." When they had done so, they caught such a large number of fish that their nets began to break. So they signaled their partners in the other boat to come and help them, and they came and filled both boats so full that they began to sink.

When Simon Peter saw this, he fell at Jesus' knees and said, "Go away from me, Lord; I am a sinful man!" For he and all his companions were astonished at the catch of fish they had taken, and so were James and John, the sons of Zebedee, Simon's partners.

Then Jesus said to Simon, "Don't be afraid; from now on you will catch men." So they pulled their boats up on shore, left everything and followed him.

....

A Moment to Reflect

Have you ever experienced a time when you were acting as if you believed, but you really didn't? What did that feel like?

Peter experienced fear only after Jesus did a miracle. Why?

Jesus calmed Peter's fears by accepting him. God accepts you.

Jesus also calmed Peter's fears by calling him to serve others. God also calls you to serve.

Spend time reflecting on how much God loves and accepts you. Talk with Him about your fears. Ask God to show you who He would like you to serve today.

When you're in the midst of a storm, it's hard to see anything. How does this image speak to you?

EXPECTING A PERFECT LIFE

A Simple Thought

On September 1, 2005, just two days after Hurricane Katrina devastated the city of New Orleans, the Associated Press reported this story:

> Set down on dry land for the first time in three days, 83-year-old Camille Fletcher stumbled a few feet to a brick wall and collapsed. She and two of her children had made it through Hurricane Katrina alive, but her Glendalyn with the long, beautiful black hair was gone.
>
> "My precious daughter," she sobbed Wednesday. "I prayed to God to keep us safe in his loving care." Then, looking into an incongruously blue sky, she whimpered: "You're supposed to be a loving God. You're supposed to love us. And what have you done to us? Why did you do this to us?"[1]

Camille Fletcher said out loud what many of us feel when we face unexpected suffering. In the midst of a storm, we cry to God to help us, to save us. At times, God does save us, and at other times tragedy strikes. Even in her anger and sadness, Camille expressed her faith and frustration with God.

The disciples expected that if they were with Jesus, nothing could go wrong. Yet one afternoon as they rowed across the sea, a violent storm came up. They feared for their lives. Jesus, on the other hand, slept through it. Didn't He care that they were in danger?

After waking up, Jesus calmed the storm and left the disciples filled with fear and amazement.

God has all power over nature and yet He still allows storms to happen. By His actions, Jesus teaches the disciples that He is in control, even in the midst of a storm. God's presence with us doesn't mean that a storm will never batter us. Rather, Jesus' presence with us can bring peace in the midst of questions and chaos.

As you read this story of Jesus, pray that God will help you to understand who He is and who He created you to be.

God's Word for You Today: Luke 8:22-25

One day Jesus said to his disciples, "Let's go over to the other side of the lake." So they got into a boat and set out. As they sailed, he fell asleep. A squall came down on the lake, so that the boat was being swamped, and they were in great danger.

The disciples went and woke him, saying, "Master, Master, we're going to drown!"

He got up and rebuked the wind and the raging waters; the storm subsided, and all was calm. "Where is your faith?" he asked his disciples. In fear and amazement they asked one another, "Who is this? He commands even the winds and the water, and they obey him."

Note
1. Allen G. Breed, "Rescuers Race to Locate Stranded, Dying People," the Associated Press (September 1, 2005).

A Moment to Reflect

....

God is with us in suffering, but He doesn't always remove our suffering. How does knowing that God is with you bring comfort?

With the knowledge that we're all vulnerable to nature's wrath, what are your fears? Would you rather face those fears with or without God?

Each day, there are those in this world who suffer without the knowledge of God's care. Take time today to pray that those who are hurting may know the peace of Jesus Christ.

Consider how God will provide for you as you reflect on His glory.

A Simple Thought

Fear keeps us from loving others.

"If I help too many people, I will not have enough to provide for myself or my family."

"If I give money to homeless people, how do I know they won't just get high?"

"If I reach out to befriend that new person at work or school, I might get smothered; after all, I don't have very much free time anyway."

We're afraid that our money, time and other resources are so scarce that we need to protect what we have. We believe that God helps those who help themselves, so when faced with someone else's need we figure they should provide for themselves. We fear not having enough, even when we have more than enough for our daily needs.

Jesus offers us an alternative. His words warn us not to let our fear of not having enough control us. Rather, he encourages us to trust God with what we have. When we do, we can leave fear behind. We don't have to worry when we understand that God is not only able to provide for us but that He also wants to provide for our needs.

How do we know that God will provide? When we slow down long enough to consider God's creation. We can experience God's provision when we sit quietly on an isolated beach, or in a wooded forest, or perhaps in a field of flowers.

As you read the following words of Jesus, pray that God will help you to understand who He is and who He created you to be.

God's Word for You Today: Luke 12:22-34, *RSV*

And he said to his disciples, "Therefore I tell you, do not be anxious about your life, what you shall eat, nor about your body, what you shall put on. For life is more than food, and the body more than clothing. Consider the ravens: they neither sow nor reap, they have neither storehouse nor barn, and yet God feeds them. Of how much more value are you than the birds! And which of you by being anxious can add a cubit to his span of life? If then you are not able to do as small a thing as that, why are you anxious about the rest?

"Consider the lilies, how they grow; they neither toil nor spin; yet I tell you, even Solomon in all his glory was not arrayed like one of these. But if God so clothes the grass which is alive in the field today and tomorrow is thrown into the oven, how much more will he clothe you, O men of little faith! And do not seek what you are to eat and what you are to drink, nor be of anxious mind. For all the nations of the world seek these things; and your Father knows that you need them. Instead, seek his kingdom, and these things shall be yours as well.

"Fear not, little flock, for it is your Father's good pleasure to give you the kingdom. Sell your possessions, and give alms; provide yourselves with purses that do not grow old, with a treasure in the heavens that does not fail, where no thief approaches and no moth destroys. For where your treasure is, there will your heart be also."

A Moment to Reflect

As you consider Jesus' words, think about what it would take for you to trust God with every aspect of your life.

Read this Scripture passage once more, aloud, and consider whether what Jesus is saying is true. If true, what are the implications for your life? If not true, think about why you don't believe.

Take time to speak to God about Jesus' words, and allow God to speak to you about your fears and where you place your trust.

God pulls you into situations, and He stays with you.
As you enter into new situations today, imagine God being with you wherever you go.

FEAR OF THE FUTURE

A Simple Thought

In 2005, world-class surf photographer Larry Moore, known as Flame, lost his battle with brain cancer. As his death approached, Larry experienced peace. He was not afraid to die.

The surf community wondered how this man who loved life so deeply could face his death so calmly. It was simple: Flame's love for the surf ran a close second to his first love—God. He knew that God was with him, and he had no need to fear his future demise.

At his death, however, others mourned deeply.

Nobody likes to lose a friend. We want the ones we love to be always with us. The thought of someone close to us dying, or even moving away, can seem unbearable. Many of us experience our first loss when a family member dies or a friend moves away. If our parents divorce, it can feel as if a part of us has died.

All of us will eventually face loss and change, and the fear of being alone.

God knows that fear. He also did something about it.

Most of the disciples walked with Jesus for about three years. His leadership, friendship and love literally changed their lives. He became their shelter in the midst of a storm. When Jesus told them He was leaving them, they didn't understand, and they were afraid.

Jesus promised to send a spiritual counselor—the Holy Spirit—to be with His friends. The Holy Spirit has been called to come alongside those who seek God. What if you could have a friend, with tremendous power and love, who was willing and able to always be there for you?

Do you want to know God's presence today?

As you read these words of Jesus from Scripture, pray that God will help you to understand who He is and experience the peace He offers you even in the midst of change.

God's Word for You Today: John 14:1-7,25-27

....

"Do not let your hearts be troubled. Trust in God; trust also in me. In my Father's house are many rooms; if it were not so, I would have told you. I am going there to prepare a place for you. And if I go and prepare a place for you, I will come back and take you to be with me that you also may be where I am. You know the way to the place where I am going."

Thomas said to him, "Lord, we don't know where you are going, so how can we know the way?"

Jesus answered, "I am the way and the truth and the life. No one comes to the Father except through me. If you really knew me, you would know my Father as well. From now on, you do know him and have seen him.

"All this I have spoken while still with you. But the Counselor, the Holy Spirit, whom the Father will send in my name, will teach you all things and will remind you of everything I have said to you. Peace I leave with you; my peace I give you. I do not give to you as the world gives. Do not let your hearts be troubled and do not be afraid."

....

A Moment to Reflect

How does the knowledge that God is with you help you face any fear of the future?

Have you ever had an experience in which you felt God's Spirit giving you peace or comfort or direction?

The way to experience the peace of God is through Jesus Christ. If you haven't already done so, ask Jesus into your heart today so that you might know the fullness of God's peace.

Sometimes you need to stand alone with God. Do you sense God calling you to take a stand today?

NOT AFRAID TO SPEAK UP

....

A Simple Thought

All that is necessary for the triumph of evil is for good people to do nothing.
- Edmund Burke -

We often hesitate when we feel called to speak a word of truth in a dangerous situation. Although we know that we should speak out when we see evil being done, many times we remain silent.

We're afraid to get involved. We're afraid that we might say the wrong thing. We're afraid that we could make the situation worse.

Here's the truth: God calls us to stand publicly against evil. He may not remove our fear, but He will be with us as we confront those fears. We can stand up against evil because God has power over evil.

One of the most influential Christians in the first century was the apostle Paul. He spoke to all kinds of people about God's love—to rulers, the poor and everyone in between. When you speak to that many people, you eventually make someone mad.

While Paul continually encouraged everyone to follow Christ, other religious leaders wanted to control how people lived their lives. Some were so angry with Paul's message that they wanted to kill Paul simply because he told the truth about God's love. Paul had to make a choice—to continue to speak the truth or to walk away.

Read about how God spoke to Paul when he was afraid, and pray that God would help you to understand who He is and how God is calling you to live.

....

God's Word for You Today: Acts 18:7-11

....

Then Paul left the synagogue and went next door to the house of Titius Justus, a worshiper of God. Crispus, the synagogue ruler, and his entire household believed in the Lord; and many of the Corinthians who heard him believed and were baptized.

One night the Lord spoke to Paul in a vision: "Do not be afraid; keep on speaking, do not be silent. For I am with you, and no one is going to attack and harm you, because I have many people in this city." So Paul stayed for a year and a half, teaching them the word of God.

....

A Moment to Reflect

....

God promised to protect Paul, so Paul felt free to speak the truth about God's love. God will protect you, too. Take a moment to pray for someone who is hurting and lost. What fears do you have about telling others about God?

Silently meditate on God's words to Paul. If God were speaking to you, what do you think He would say to you right now? Ask God to give you an opportunity to talk about Him today.

....

....

A Simple Thought

Imagine if you were going through some old files at home and you found a letter from a lawyer's office postmarked July 12, 1996. You began thinking about the past nine years of your life: You had lost your job, your marriage was struggling because of money problems and you had begun to have a few drinks every night to calm your nerves.

Imagine your surprise when after opening the letter you read that you had been left an inheritance of $500,000. All you had to do was call the lawyer's office to retrieve the details and claim your money. You'd been living with fear about finances for a long time when all you had to do was open a letter.

Does it ever feel like you can't seem to get your life together? Do you get frustrated because you don't know where your life is going and you don't even know how to start making plans?

Do you ever feel as if everything is working against you?

You've been given an inheritance: God has promised to be with you each day, providing strength and giving you the ability to live a life of joy. The good news is that you don't have to do anything to make God love you more; you simply need to confess that you need His help and then allow Him to work in your life. He will show you how to live!

We often feel enslaved to old attitudes and habits that keep us living in fear. The great news is that God has given you a new life; you only need to turn away from the old way of living and turn toward God's love in Jesus Christ.

As you read what Paul wrote to the church at Rome, ask God to speak to you about who He is and the inheritance He has already given you.

....

Are you ready to break free today from old habits that are bringing you down, and pursue God?

God's Word for You Today: Romans 8:12-17

....

Therefore, brothers, we have an obligation—but it is not to the sinful nature, to live according to it. For if you live according to the sinful nature, you will die; but if by the Spirit you put to death the misdeeds of the body, you will live, because those who are led by the Spirit of God are sons of God. For you did not receive a spirit that makes you a slave again to fear, but you received the Spirit of sonship. And by him we cry, "Abba, Father." The Spirit himself testifies with our spirit that we are God's children. Now if we are children, then we are heirs—heirs of God and co-heirs with Christ, if indeed we share in his sufferings in order that we may also share in his glory.

....

A Moment to Reflect

In what ways have your old habits and attitudes kept you from experiencing the life that God has for you? Describe some ways a Christian would share in Christ's suffering and then feel God's presence.

As you pray today, ask God to show you areas in your life that He would like to change so that you might experience the full joy of being His child.

Sometimes we go too far. Have you found yourself experiencing the results of a bad decision lately?

A Simple Thought

"Shhh! Quiet in the library." "No skating on the steps." "Sir, you were driving 15 miles over the speed limit—let me see your license and registration." "That miniskirt is a violation of school dress code, young lady."

We've all experienced others telling us what to do. Whether it's a teacher, a parent, a police officer or our boss at work, we often find ourselves resentful and rebellious when they say something to control our behavior.

We want to believe that our attitude toward authority figures has nothing to do with God. (Who are they to tell us how to live? It's not like they're agents of God or anything!)

Or are they?

The apostle Paul wrote to the church in Rome that rebelling against authority isn't an option for those who want to honor God. Why? Because the authorities are, in fact, agents of God, put in our lives to do us good, even when we think the rules are unfair.

Jennifer had gotten caught going through a red light by a camera set up at an intersection in her town. Frustrated by having to pay a fine, she railed against the cameras. "I'm a good driver—it was just that one time." But after a few weeks of slamming on the brakes at every intersection and continually being afraid of getting caught by the cameras, she had to admit that possibly she wasn't giving herself enough time to stop at intersections.

Once she slowed down and paid more attention to her driving, her fear of getting caught by the cameras and getting another fine began to subside.

We can end up living in fear when we allow ourselves to rebel and break the rules. It doesn't seem like a big problem at the beginning, but eventually we feel like we're always looking over our shoulder.

God desires to set us free from those fears. He sets authorities in our lives to help keep us headed in the right direction. He desires to transform our rebellious hearts and give us peace as we strive to follow Him and give Him honor.

As you read and meditate on the Scripture, ask God to open your heart and mind and help you hear what He wants to say to you today.

God's Word for You Today: Romans 13:1-5

....

Everyone must submit himself to the governing authorities, for there is no authority except that which God has established. The authorities that exist have been established by God. Consequently, he who rebels against the authority is rebelling against what God has instituted, and those who do so will bring judgment on themselves. For rulers hold no terror for those who do right, but for those who do wrong. Do you want to be free from fear of the one in authority? Then do what is right and he will commend you. For he is God's servant to do you good. But if you do wrong, be afraid, for he does not bear the sword for nothing. He is God's servant, an agent of wrath to bring punishment to the wrongdoer. Therefore, it is necessary to submit to the authorities, not only because of possible punishment but also because of conscience.

....

A Moment to Reflect

When have you ever felt like you were living life by having to look over your shoulder? What would it feel like to leave the fear of being found out behind you? Talk to God and tell Him about the parts of your life that you're not proud of. What might happen if you were to invite God to transform your heart?

Do you ever feel as though you don't have enough for the task you are facing?

FREEDOM FROM MONEY WORRIES

A Simple Thought

Most of us will never face the extreme situation of having our home blown up by a bomb. But others throughout the world do face this fear or have faced this fear. Check out this story from England in the 1940s:

> During the bombing raids of World War II, thousands of children were orphaned and left to starve. The fortunate ones were rescued and placed in refugee camps where they were fed and cared for. But many of these children who had lost so much could not sleep at night. They feared waking up to find themselves once again homeless and without food. Nothing seemed to reassure them. Finally, someone hit upon the idea of giving each child a piece of bread to hold at bedtime. Holding their bread, these children could finally sleep in peace. All through the night the bread reminded them, "Today I ate and I will eat again tomorrow."[1]

Have you ever experienced a sleepless night because you were worried about how you were going to provide for yourself or for others you love? The clock reads 2:00 A.M., and your mind replays images of your worries like a bad loop you can't shut off.

We experience anxiety when we feel like we don't have enough. A lack of money, especially, produces fear and even panic. If we're honest, many of us feel that if we just had enough money, the rest of our lives would be okay. Pictures of the rich and famous give the impression that having enough money will relieve much of the stress of life.

When the English children in WW II held on to a piece of bread at night, they were reassured that everything would be all right.

You, too, can sleep without worry. You have much more than a simple piece of bread. You have the promise that God will never abandon you. As you sleep each night, imagine God in your room, giving you His word that all you need will be provided.

In a sermon written in the first century, the preacher reminded his church that God was with them. Before you read a part of that sermon, take a moment to pray that God will speak to you about the fears you experience because of money.

God's Word for You Today: Hebrews 13:5-6

Keep your lives free from the love of money and be content with what you have, because God has said, "Never will I leave you; never will I forsake you."

So we say with confidence,

"The Lord is my helper, I will not be afraid. What can man do to me?"

{ A Moment to Reflect }

Think about these words: "The Lord is my helper, I will not be afraid. What can man do to me?"
How does God as your helper change the worries you have today?
Do you love to have money, or are you content with your situation? Reflect on ways that you can keep your life free from the love of money.
Giving to someone else can help you live without fear. Often, people will give money and possessions away as a way to remind themselves that God will always provide. Pray that God will give you an opportunity today to give away some money to someone who is in need.

Note
1. Dennis Linn, et al, *Sleeping with Bread* (Mahwah, NY: Paulist Press, 1995), p. 1.

Others will often watch when you decide to take on a new challenge. What opportunities have you been given to show others how to enjoy God's creation?

....

A Simple Thought

We live in a world in which evil seeks to stop others from doing good.

Martin Luther King, Jr. was killed for trying to help African-Americans have the same civil rights as others in America.

Gangs in New Orleans fired shots at rescue workers who were trying to deliver food and fix levees in the aftermath of Hurricane Katrina.

Jesus was killed when He told others about God's kingdom.

The world has always been that way. The first Christians experienced persecution when they tried to love their neighbors and care for those who were hurting. They were accused of being cannibals when they talked about the Body and Blood of Christ. They were also arrested for being atheists, because they didn't believe in all the gods of the Roman pantheon. Some were put to death. Some were put in jail. Some were isolated from their neighbors.

As you seek to live a fearless life, trusting in God, you'll find that others will be both intrigued and annoyed. They will wonder how you can believe in a God when so many bad things happen in the world. They will also wonder why you don't exhibit the same stress they have when they face hard situations.

How will you respond?

As you read the Scripture passage that was written to those first Christians, ask God to show you more about who He is and how God has called you to live.

....

God's Word for You Today: 1 Peter 3:13-18

....

Who is going to harm you if you are eager to do good? But even if you should suffer for what is right, you are blessed. "Do not fear what they fear; do not be frightened." But in your hearts set apart Christ as Lord. Always be prepared to give an answer to everyone who asks you to give the reason for the hope that you have. But do this with gentleness and respect, keeping a clear conscience, so that those who speak maliciously against your good behavior in Christ may be ashamed of their slander. It is better, if it is God's will, to suffer for doing good than for doing evil. For Christ died for sins once for all, the righteous for the unrighteous, to bring you to God. He was put to death in the body but made alive by the Spirit.

....

A Moment to Reflect

Reflect on a time when you experienced or saw someone being persecuted for doing good. When you've been accused or put down, how did you respond? How would your life change if you saw all people as children who are loved by God?

How can your life be an example for others of the grace and love of God today?

As you pray, reflect on what sins God has forgiven in your life. Ask God to show you how to share that love with others today.

God is love. Do you sense freedom in this image? Why? Do you sense fear?

NO FEAR IN LOVE

A Simple Thought

God created you to live with others. God designed you to enjoy being with people and working together. When we love, you and the world are living as God intends.

God loves you. You can now love others.

When we know love, we have no need to fear.

When we no longer fear, we can live in such a way that God's love is seen in us.

When we live out God's love, the world will change for the better.

When the world changes for the better, others will see God.

When others see God, they will have no need to fear.

For the past 36 days, you've been reading about fear. At the same time, you've actually been reflecting on love. Fear and love are intimately connected. In fact, the opposite of love is fear. Fear breads hate, unforgiveness, rage and apathy. Because we are afraid, we seek to separate ourselves from God and from others.

When we experience love, when we know that we have all that we need, we can effectively care for others.

Take a moment to reflect on God's love. John, the man who wrote our passage today, lived the longest of all the disciples. He lived through Jesus' death and the death of his friends, and at the end of his life, he reflected on one thing: the love of God.

Before you read this passage, ask God to reveal to you the profound love He has for you and for the world.

If anyone acknowledges that Jesus is the Son of God, God lives in him and he in God. And so we know and rely on the love God has for us. God is love. Whoever lives in love lives in God, and God in him. In this way, love is made complete among us so that we will have confidence on the day of judgment, because in this world we are like him. There is no fear in love. But perfect love drives out fear, because fear has to do with punishment. The one who fears is not made perfect in love.

We love because he first loved us. If anyone says, "I love God," yet hates his brother, he is a liar. For anyone who does not love his brother, whom he has seen, cannot love God, whom he has not seen. And he has given us this command: Whoever loves God must also love his brother.

A Moment to Reflect

Jesus said that the two greatest commandments were to love God and love your neighbor. God calls us to live our lives trusting Him in all things. You've been created to love God and actively love your friends, neighbors, and relatives. Will you follow that call?

As you pray this morning, take time to read this passage again slowly. Allow the words to sink deeply into your soul. You may want to write down the phrases that speak to you and use them throughout the day as a guide.

How does this image remind you that God will be with you today?

A Simple Thought

Would you prefer to explore the jungles of Brazil for the first time on your own or with a guide who could point out both the dangers and the wonders?

Would you prefer to surf a new reef break on your own or with someone who knows the jagged bottom from years of experience?

Would you prefer to navigate a new school on your own or with someone friendly to walk with you to show you the way around campus?

Would you prefer to experience life on your own or with the One who has been guiding individuals from the beginning of time?

You may not know your future, but you can know the One who holds your future in His loving hands.

Some people believe that God created the universe, set it in motion and then sat back to watch us live our lives, as if He were watching a dramatic comedy. That thinking says, God may have created everything, but we are left to work out the details. And if life becomes overwhelming, we simply need to work a little harder and handle whatever situation we've been given.

When the apostle John ended up in prison because he told others about Christ, his life was out of his control. Then God gave him a vision.

John confronted a terrifying thought: *What if this life is all there is?* What if we are truly alone? In the vision, God showed up, placed his hand on John's shoulder and assured him that everything was under control—he didn't need to be afraid. God has been holding things together from the very beginning and will do so to the very end.

The one who came to Earth as a man and died on a cross is the one who holds the power of life and death. He's the one who loves you, the one who guides you through the trials of life and eventually welcomes you in your death.

You truly have no need to fear.

Before you read this passage, ask God to reveal to you the profound love He has for you and for the world.

God's Word for You Today: Revelation 1:17-18

When I saw him, I fell at his feet as though dead. Then he placed his right hand on me and said: "Do not be afraid. I am the First and the Last. I am the Living One; I was dead, and behold I am alive for ever and ever! And I hold the keys of death and Hades."

A Moment to Reflect

....

Have you ever felt the comfort of a friend placing a hand on your shoulder when you were afraid or overwhelmed? Imagine God placing His hand on your shoulder. Tell Him about your day.

Facing death will be everyone's greatest challenge. Do you find comfort in knowing that God has control even over death?

Jesus Christ was God coming to Earth as the ambassador from heaven to guide you in this life and the next. Would you like Him to be your guide? It all begins by asking Him to help you face your next challenge.

....

Sometimes a walk with God can feel nice and clean. Sometimes it can feel ugly. God is with you always. Will you seek Him today?

NO FEAR IN DEATH   Day 39

A Simple Thought

When explorers and others from Europe introduced the disease of leprosy to the native people of the Hawaiian Islands, those who contracted the disease were quarantined from the rest of the population by being taken on boats and dropped overboard near the island of Molokai.

These men and women had no hope. They simply waited to die.

In 1873, a priest asked to work with the lepers on the desolate island of Molokai. Known as Father Damien, Joseph Van Vuester began to treat those who had leprosy with dignity and love. He honored them when they died with a proper funeral. He also helped organize their communities by teaching them to grow their own food and to eat properly. He served as a doctor, and he personally washed their wounds.

When he first came to the island, not many people attended church. After showing God's love through his actions, people began to flock to church to hear about a God who loved them. Father Damien dedicated his life to people who had literally been thrown away by the world.

Father Damien eventually died of leprosy on Molokai. His fearless love for God and for others caused people to see and know God. In his death, he found the peace that he offered to so many others.

God spoke some encouraging words to a church in the first century. As you read these words, consider how God might be calling you to live a life of no fear.

God's Word for You Today: Revelation 2:8-11

....

To the angel of the church in Smyrna write:

These are the words of him who is the First and the Last, who died and came to life again. I know your afflictions and your poverty—yet you are rich! I know the slander of those who say they are Jews and are not, but are a synagogue of Satan. Do not be afraid of what you are about to suffer. I tell you, the devil will put some of you in prison to test you, and you will suffer persecution for ten days. Be faithful, even to the point of death, and I will give you the crown of life. He who has an ear, let him hear what the Spirit says to the churches. He who overcomes will not be hurt at all by the second death.

....

A Moment to Reflect

A life with God doesn't mean a life without pain or suffering. In fact, sometimes God allows us to suffer so that others might live. What thoughts do you have when you hear the story of Father Damien? Read once more through the Scripture passage from Revelation. What part of this passage do you find encouraging? What do you find frightening?

Have you ever known anyone who lived a rich life, though he or she was poor in the world's eyes?

When you find what you are looking for, there is no need for fear.
You will experience great joy.

NO FEAR, GOD IS HERE

....

A Simple Thought

Valentine James Stephen traveled across the Atlantic Ocean in 1926, looking for his father. Despite the uncertainty about his future, this 14-year-old set out from Poland ready for adventure. He carried with him a suitcase, a bottle of wine and a loaf of bread.

Val's father, a farmer who lived in poverty with his family, had moved to the United States years before, looking for a new land and a new life. His search brought them hope.

Eventually, Valentine came looking for his father with the hope of finding something better, too.

A life without fear begins when we return to our Father and reunite with the one who loves us deeply. At creation, God walked with a man and woman in a garden. God's garden provided everything the man and woman needed. When they separated from God, they experienced the darkness of fear and began a quest to find security and peace.

The Bible begins with this great separation and ends with a great reunion. In the midst of fear, in the midst of uncertainty, in the midst of the day-to-day grind, a constant promise echoes through the biblical message: *You do not need to fear; God is near*.

One day that promise will be fulfilled. John, the friend of Jesus, who had a vision of heaven, gave us a great first-century photograph of what heaven will look like. In the center of heaven sits God, with the Lamb giving light to the whole earth. Literally, the light of God has removed all fear.

As you read the Scripture passage today, ask God to give you a vision of His hope for your life.

....

God's Word for You Today: Revelation 22:1-7, *RSV*

Then he showed me the river of the water of life, bright as crystal, flowing from the throne of God and of the Lamb through the middle of the street of the city; also, on either side of the river, the tree of life with its twelve kinds of fruit, yielding its fruit each month; and the leaves of the tree were for the healing of the nations. There shall no more be anything accursed, but the throne of God and of the Lamb shall be in it, and his servants shall worship him; they shall see his face, and his name shall be on their foreheads. And night shall be no more; they need no light of lamp or sun, for the Lord God will be their light, and they shall reign for ever and ever. And he said to me, "These words are trustworthy and true. And the Lord, the God of the spirits of the prophets, has sent his angel to show his servants what must soon take place. And behold, I am coming soon." Blessed is he who keeps the words of the prophecy of this book.

A Moment to Reflect

What are your thoughts and feelings as you consider this image of heaven?
How does knowing that one day all the evil and hurt in the world will be removed make you feel?
Have you grown closer to God during the past 40 days? What has made a difference?
Will you continue to seek God?